HIP
HOTELS
PARIS

HERBERT YPMA

HIP
HOTELS
PARIS

with 304 illustrations, 224 in color

Thames & Hudson

contents

what is HIP?

Travel has changed. No corner of the world is unfamiliar anymore; globetrotting has become decidedly more democratic; cut-price air fares make almost any destination possible; and the easing of border bureaucracy has undoubtedly made things less of a hurdle.

What this means is that we are now free to pursue experiences on a more individual level; to seek out destinations that strike a personal note in terms of architecture, location, ambience and design – destinations that make us think, 'Now that's my kind of place.'

And that, from the very beginning, has been the point of HIP HOTELS; to find and share unique, authentic, inspiring places that will make you simply want to 'pack a bag and go'. And you can go secure in the knowledge that there have been no short-cuts taken. Each hotel featured is one that I have stayed in myself and photographed. That's your assurance and guarantee that all the hotels in this book are truly **H**ighly **I**ndividual **P**laces.

Herbert Ypma

introduction

'To know Paris is to know a great deal.' Henry Miller

There are countless quotes from countless writers, famous and infamous, but perhaps this pared-down gem from Henry Miller says it all. Of all the cities in the world that offer the potential of revelation – to see, to visit, to experience something that you wouldn't at home, wherever you may come from – Paris offers the most.

Not only is it bewitchingly beautiful but it's also magically hedonistic. This is not a tour-bus type of city. It's a walk-around, sit-in-a-café, eat-with-abandon and watch-the-world-go-by type of city. And unlike Venice, it's not dedicated to tourism. The city belongs to Parisians and, like them or hate them, they give this monumental collection of mid-millennium French history the character and pizzazz that animate a place.

Paris is still one of those cities that will show you a different way of life but also encourage you to experience it for yourself while you're there. Buying a baguette, ordering a *café crème*, taking the *plat du jour*, going for a stroll in formal gardens, stopping for an *apéritif* ... these are the true pleasures of Paris. All that is left to do is to choose where you will indulge in these things, and which museums, galleries or shops you might visit in between.

If you know this, then you too will know a great deal.

1st arrondissement

They call it the *premier*, or first, *arrondissement*, and for good reason. It's one of the largest and, certainly from a historical perspective, most important, areas of Paris. Almost every monument you can think of is here. At one end there's the Place de la Concorde, with its 3,000-year-old obelisk. At the other end there's the Louvre, the world's largest and most famous museum. Originally built as a fortified castle by Philippe Auguste, it was torn down by François I and rebuilt as an elegant palace. Subsequent rulers have all made their mark: Henri IV added a long wing along the Seine, Louis XIV finished the courtyard that François I started, Napoleon Bonaparte constructed the wings that border the rue de Rivoli, and by the time Napoleon III had finished his great-uncle's work, the Louvre had been under construction for three hundred years. If you add Mitterrand's addition of I. M. Pei's glass pyramid, the project has lasted more than four hundred years.

Part of the area's prestige derives from the fact that it was long the centre of power. Even when the French court moved to Versailles, the area around the Tuileries and the Louvre remained the King's Paris … which explains why figures like Cardinal Richelieu built his palace, now known as the Palais Royal, in close proximity. It also explains why Napoleon chose Place Vendôme for his splendid column, made entirely from melted-down enemy cannons.

In true Parisian fashion, not much has changed. Institutions such as the Ritz and the Hôtel Meurice are here in the 1st. Perhaps leaders are no longer building monuments for the aristocratic residents, but large French luxury companies are certainly using rue Faubourg Saint-Honoré as their upmarket showcase. If you have an affinity with France's 'rich' heritage, the 1st is definitely the address for you.

costes

When the Costes first opened it was quite a phenomenon. It was *the* place to be seen for breakfast, lunch and dinner. All *le beau monde* of Paris – from the worlds of film, fashion, television, music and publishing – made it their hangout. Even other hotels recommended it as a place to eat out – if you could get a table, that is.

This success was vindication for designer Jacques Garcia and his visionary client Jean-Louis Costes. Until Garcia came along, the style of the late nineteenth-century Belle Epoque was generally disdained by serious critics of the French decorative arts. It was considered too busy, too confused: too much colour, too many patterns and too many disparate influences – Rococo, neo-Gothic, Empire and Orientalism among them. But that is exactly why Garcia used it as his design theme. For his style preferences are the exact opposite of the modern trend towards simplicity. For him too much is *never* enough.

The chairs, the lamps, the carpets, the fabrics, even the classical statues that adorn the courtyard were specially designed and made for the hotel. In an age when we are increasingly accustomed to urban colour schemes of white and more white, Garcia saturated the interior with strong, rich, luxurious shades. Bathrooms are painted deep earthy reds or strong ochre yellows, floors are tiled in Moorish patterns, chairs are upholstered in rich red silks patterned in stripes, paisleys and brocades, bedroom walls are papered in bold Victorian florals and paisleys, dining rooms are panelled in gilded wooden boiserie, bar stools – Oriental in form – are covered in studded acid-green velour. On it goes....

Perhaps it's not a decor many people would wish to live with, but then that's not the point. Costes is an adventure, a visual vacation from what you're used to. When the lights are turned down and the rich *fin de siècle* setting truly comes into its own, it's a magic place.

Jean-Louis Costes has built his hotel and restaurant empire on the most fundamental truth guiding today's hospitality industry: people don't want everything to be the same. What would be the fun of travel if it was?

address Hôtel Costes, 239 rue Saint-Honoré, 75001 Paris
tel (33) (0)1 42 44 50 00 **fax** (33) (0)1 42 44 50 01
e-mail remarks@hotelcostes.com
room rates from €500

absolutely have to see
Musée du Louvre, rue de Rivoli, 75001 Paris (tel 01 40 20 53 17): quite simply
the world's most famous museum. Just start anywhere; you'll definitely be back

must have dinner
L'Escargot Montorgueil, 38 rue Montorgueil, 75001 Paris (tel 01 42 36 83 51):
the perfect pre- or post-Louvre institution, it has served snails to the likes of
Marcel Proust, Sarah Bernhardt and Jean Cocteau since 1832

hôtel thérèse

Generally speaking, hotels in the 1st aren't cheap. Even the more cutting-edge ones, like Costes, are affordable only if the words 'vice president' or 'chief' appear somewhere on your business card. Style, value and location do not often go hand in hand here … which is what makes the Thérèse so special.

The first impression upon entering the elegantly contemporary lobby in its signature tones of camel, aubergine and ebony is of a hotel that is as chic and elite as the arrondissement it is in. Yet it is delightfully inconsistent with the area in the fact that it is surprisingly affordable. Better still, it is just around the corner from one of the most enchanting places in Paris, the Palais Royal.

Originally known as le Palais Cardinal, it was built for Louis XIII's most important minister, Cardinal Richelieu. Upon his death he bequeathed the palace to the King, hence its current epithet. No king has in fact ever lived here but many minor royals have. At one point the aristocracy remodelled the estate with a view to collecting rent: boutiques and cafés were added to the ground floor and the upper floors were converted into apartments, and so it remains today. In the great Parisian tradition of adding art to monuments, Mitterrand commissioned a vast sculpture by Daniel Buren to enhance the main courtyard: all those rows of columns of varying heights in striking black and white stone have certainly generated their fair share of controversy, but it's undisputed that they have made the Palais Royal even more layered and fascinating in its appeal. What's more, the Palais is arguably just as popular a place today for people to gather in the enclosed gardens and all the restaurants cloistered on the ground floor as it was two centuries ago.

Enjoying Paris to the full is a no-brainer at Thérèse. You wake in a stylishly elegant guest room painted in sophisticated shades of greyish blues or absinthe greens. You wander down the classic winding oak staircase to take 'petit dej' (breakfast) in the 'cave' (cellar), and from there the Louvre, the gardens of the Tuileries, the famous bridges across the Seine, as well as shops on elegant Faubourg Saint-Honoré, are within easy walking distance.

The twist in all this is that the proprietor and designer of the hotel, Madame Sylvie de Lattre, is a bit of an Anglophile, and she created Thérèse in the image of the comfortable, stylish (and affordable) hotels she had found in the British countryside. It's not her fault that she did it with such French style. She is a Parisienne after all....

address Hôtel Thérèse, 5–7 rue Thérèse, 75001 Paris
tel (33) (0)1 42 96 10 01   **fax** (33) (0)1 42 96 15 22
e-mail info@hoteltherese.com
room rates from €134

absolutely have to see
The Palais Royal, Place du Palais-Royal, 75001 Paris: a slice of intact 18th-century Paris to experience unchanged except for Daniel Buren's controversial sculpture installation

must have dinner
Le Grand Véfour, 17 rue de Beaujolais, 75001 Paris (tel 01 42 96 56 27): think gilded mirrors and chandeliers, set in the splendid arcades of the Palais Royal

le marais

Literally translated, 'le marais' means 'the swamp' – a strange name for one of the oldest and most historic quarters of Paris…. Long before the days of the Louvre, the crème de la crème of Parisian society, including the royal family, lived in the area. It would have been quite a sight: the odd high wall and impressively grand door of a nobleman's *hôtel particulier* (literally townhouse, but city palace would be more accurate) amid a pungent, heady mix of little shops and filthy hovels on either side of narrow, higgledy-piggledy lanes and alleyways.

After the royals moved up the river to the splendid new Louvre, with its equally splendid Jardin des Tuileries, the nobility was obliged to do likewise, and slowly, inexorably, Le Marais turned into a slum. For 250 years it was known as the city's Jewish quarter. While other parts of Paris were razed in the nineteenth century to make way for Baron Haussmann's grand

boulevards and broad avenues, the medieval labyrinth of Le Marais was allowed to stay, only because it wasn't deemed worthy of the expense involved in tearing it down.

Today a new generation of Parisians are delighted it was ignored for so long. All those tiny buildings now suit cutting-edge boutiques, bars, cafés and hotels, and the uniquely convoluted chaos has helped make Le Marais the hippest and liveliest neighbourhood in town. It's the only area in Paris where you can shop on a Sunday, and where people are out on the streets at all hours. You may need a map to find your way around the *quartier*, but that's all part of its charm.

Now about that name. Perhaps predictably Le Marais was indeed once a swamp. It was drained but, with that twist of inverted snobbery that prefers to call a city palace a townhouse, the old name was kept.

du petit moulin

If one little building sums up the entire zeitgeist of the Marais it has to be this former *boulangerie* on tiny rue du Poitou. Legend has it that Victor Hugo used to wander up the rue de Turenne from his home on the Place des Vosges to buy his bread here. In fact the shop, with its elegantly Venetian-style interior, has the distinction of having been the oldest bakery in Paris: until recently it had been selling brioche since the time of King Henri IV.

Fascinating history is one essential ingredient of the Marais's attraction. Behind this shop-front, however, now protected as a *monument historique*, there is another chapter in full swing: the emergence of the Marais's unique sense of style. Streetwise, hip, eclectic, modern and multi-ethnic, this part of Paris is at once the city's least pretentious and most fashionable area. Creativity, not conformity, is the mantra; an anti-bourgeois groundswell that promotes 'cool' over 'grand'.

In this context it's not surprising that Nadia Murano, Denis Nourry and Jean-François Demorge – a very 'Marais' entrepreneurial trio – approached fashion name Christian Lacroix to design and decorate the Hôtel du Petit Moulin. Lacroix lives in the Marais and he is typical of its personality: 'a mix', as he puts it, 'of every trend' … which, as a soundbite, goes a long way towards describing his approach to the hotel's seventeen guest rooms.

In Lacroix's words, the rooms are 'seventeen ambiences that correspond to seventeen ways of enjoying the Marais': the 'rustic' Marais of toile de Jouy, the 'historical' Marais of wooden beams and damask, the 'Zen' Marais, and so on. Modern lamps, Venetian mirrors, flowers, stripes, antique gold, fluorescent green, slate, faience, polka dots, black lacquer.… Variety with a vengeance.

The result is surprisingly harmonious and soothing. Lacroix relates the approach to fashion. 'It's like couture,' he says, 'where the harmony is created from a puzzle of inspirations.' And what a delightful puzzle Du Petit Moulin has turned out to be.

Apart from the area, which could easily qualify for the next Roman Polanski film in terms of charm and authenticity, the hotel is like a chocolate box of the highest quality. As a guest, you have no idea what kind of room you might end up with, but one thing is certain: it will be exotic, different, unexpected and delicious. In addition, despite its couture pedigree, the hotel is surprisingly affordable. Just as well the owners are planning a few more....

address Hôtel du Petit Moulin, 29–31 rue du Poitou, 75003 Paris
tel (33) (0)1 42 74 10 10   **fax** (33) (0)1 42 74 10 97
e-mail contact@hoteldupetitmoulin.com
room rates from €180

absolutely have to see
Musée National Picasso, Hôtel Salé, 5 rue de Thorigny, 75003 Paris (tel 01 42 71 25 21): hundreds of paintings, drawings, sculptures and ceramics in an extraordinary palace dedicated to Picasso's creative legacy

must have lunch
Café Baci, 36 rue de Turenne, 75003 Paris (tel 01 42 71 36 70): a combination of great food, great design and high glamour

murano

Take one-third *Mission Impossible*, one-third Miami 'Art Basel' and one-third *Austin Powers*. Mix vigorously and put the results on the boundary of the Marais. Add a touch of French obsession with cuisine, and you have the first high-tech, high-art, high-design, high-cuisine hotel in Paris. With the Murano (named after the Venetian island that produces the distinctively cut and coloured glass, an example of which hangs in the form of a chandelier in the reception), all traditional links with Paris seem to have been severed … except one.

In today's perfectly polished, properly restored, beautifully maintained and gloriously groomed Paris, it's easy to forget the city's twentieth-century reputation as a gritty world centre for bohemian innovation, anything-goes morality and all-around nonconformity. Adoptive Parisians such as Picasso broke down barriers in matters of art, the performer Josephine Baker challenged attitudes towards nudity, and a host of other creative types from Le Corbusier and Man Ray to Louis Armstrong and Ernest Hemingway redefined architecture, photography, music and literature. But they did all this to a backdrop that in itself did not seem particularly modern. In fact during the 1930s, when Paris was establishing its reputation as the century's hotbed of creativity, there were still more horses in the capital than motor cars.

It is this modernity within tradition that establishes Murano's Parisian credentials. In a twentieth-century sense the hotel is old-fashioned, harking back as it does to an era of fearless innovation. Interestingly, the Parisians themselves were the first to respond: the bar and restaurant are always packed with locals.

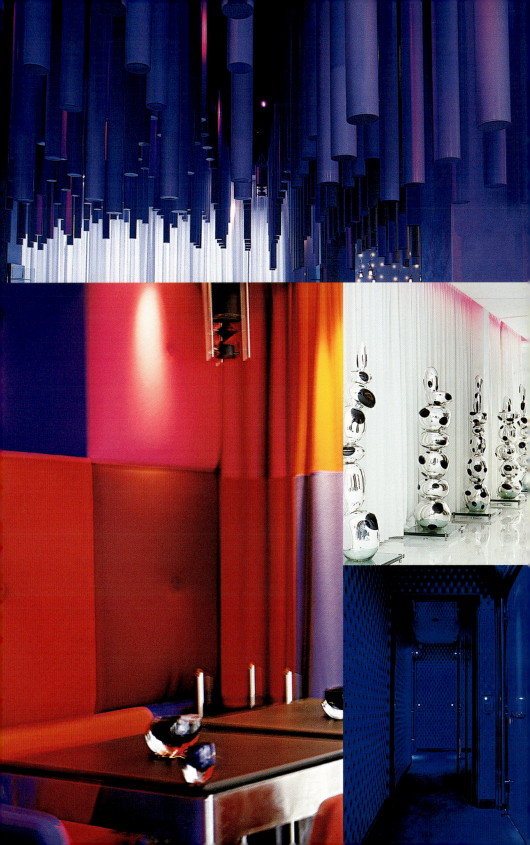

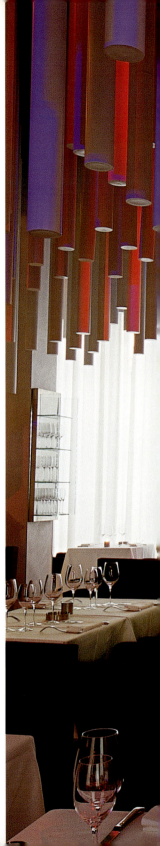

In terms of innovation, the Murano was the first hotel I know of to make use of fingerprint-recognition technology. This may not sound like a big deal, but when all you have to do to open your room is stick your finger in a scanner next to the door instead of fiddling with electronic keys that don't work or hunting for traditional keys that are always in your *other* bag, the convenience is very easy to get used to. Admittedly the use of choose-your-own-colour mood lighting in the guest rooms isn't really new, but the restaurant designed like Superman's fortress certainly is.

Nobody is suggesting that the Murano is new in every way, but any effort to rekindle Paris's reputation for groundbreaking creativity is surely reason enough to be optimistic. And let's not forget, the food is worth it, too – with or without the innovation.

address Murano Urban Resort, 13 boulevard du Temple, 75003 Paris
tel (33) (0)1 42 71 20 00 **fax** (33) (0)1 42 71 21 01
e-mail paris@muranoresort.com
room rates from €350

absolutely have to see
Canal Saint-Martin: the social centre of the nearby 11th, the canal creates an Amsterdam-like ambience in the centre of Paris, particularly poignant in summer

must have dinner
Hôtel du Nord, 102 Quai de Jemmapes, 75010 Paris (tel 01 40 40 78 78): atmospheric restaurant on the canal, immortalized in a famous French novel

pavillon de la reine

For lovers of history and authenticity, it's hard to imagine a more compelling address. Hidden behind a stone archway that connects to the signature covered walkways and elegant, four-storey façades of the legendary Place des Vosges, La Pavillon de la Reine is an ivy-covered fantasy; a mansion with its own garden courtyard in the middle of the best area of the Marais. So convincing is it in its guise as the ultimate hidden gem that every guest arrives at reception with an 'aren't I clever to have found this place?' expression on their face.

But of course they find it. The square it is on is, after all, where the aristocracy of pre-Revolutionary France used to reside. In those days, the square was known as the Place Royale, and it was often the venue for fanciful events such as jousting competitions, complete with gold-striped pomp and circumstance. The royal residents, of course, had the best views.

The Place remained the 'dernier chic' of Paris until the royals moved further up the river to the area around the Louvre and the Tuileries in the seventeenth century. Interestingly, even though the rest of the Marais slowly became a maze of shops, merchants and street hawkers, the Place Royale managed to maintain a certain decorum. It may no longer have been the address of movers and shakers but it was still prestigious enough to attract the likes of Victor Hugo as a resident in the 1800s. It helped that Napoleon Bonaparte took an interest. He loved its architecture and its history, and he rekindled attention with one of his favourite political devices: a competition. With great fanfare he announced that the first *département* in France to pay its taxes would be honoured by having the square re-named after it. Vosges paid first.

Granted, not all guests of the Pavillon de la Reine are cognisant of the enormous weight of history of the location, nor of the privilege of being able to stay in it, but frankly this isn't necessary to enjoy it. Even without historical context, it's a *très agréable* place to stay, especially since it was recently completely revamped. The exposed beams, stone walls, fireplaces and antique paintings contrast perfectly with the more contemporary red, grey and aubergine accents of the new decor, and its ambience is that of a *maison de campagne*, a country house, albeit a glamorous one, complete with appropriate peace and quiet; all a result of being so beautifully hidden away.

address Hôtel Pavillon de la Reine, 28 Place des Vosges, 75003 Paris
tel (33) (0)1 40 29 19 19 **fax** (33) (0)1 40 29 19 20
e-mail contact@pavillon-de-la-reine.com
room rates from €290

absolutely have to see
Musée Carnavalet, 23 rue de Sévigné, 75003 Paris (tel 01 44 59 58 58): the city's best collection of historic interiors, housed in one of the most sensational 16th-century mansions; a decorator's Valhalla

must have dinner
L'Ambroisie, 9 Place des Vosges, 75004 Paris (tel 01 42 78 51 45): dine by candlelight among book-lined shelves, oil paintings and Aubusson tapestries

bourg tibourg

The name rolls off the tongue in a way only French names can. It resonates with romance and Gallicness. You can almost hear Edith Piaf breathing it into a microphone in a smoky midnight jazz joint. A vowel-charged, compact bit of Frenchness, it is in fact the perfect name – and metaphor – for this hotel.

Only in Paris will you find a bolthole like this. And not just because the interior was conceived by Jacques Garcia (of Costes fame). His signature warm, sumptuous layers of decorative texture and colour recall the elegant decadence of the Belle Epoque but, in the case of Bourg Tibourg, it's the sum of the hotel's parts that makes it so special.

First there's the street. Bourg-Tibourg is probably the most charming little street in the entire Marais, not to mention the fact that it's disproportionately blessed with cafés, bars, restaurants and tea rooms. At one end is the Place du Bourg Tibourg, which is very much a focal point – the gathering place for the area's eclectic, fashionable and slightly bohemian crowd.

Then there's the hotel building – a perfect little stone-clad chocolate box with light blue shutters, ivy on the walls, a door in the middle and the world's most discreet sign; the kind of building that blends so successfully into the Marais that, were it not for the remarkably rich interior, you might walk straight past it.

The hotel's not big by any means. The reception salon and lobby spaces are small, even by Parisian standards, though this only enhances the charm of the place. And the breakfast room has been placed in the cellars, but with such style and conviction that it's like eating in a medieval castle, complete with no windows but lots of red velvet.

Then there are the stairs. In most hotels and apartment buildings, unless they are *hôtels particuliers*, staircases are hardly a decorative feature: they fall into the same category as corridors – spaces that play rather plain, utilitarian roles. Not so at Bourg Tibourg. Painted a vivid Prussian blue, the staircase with its bolt of colour and distinctively striped runner is as funky as they come. Ditto the corridors. This is a reflection of the attention to detail that permeates every corner, nook and cranny of the hotel.

This care and attention to detail reflects the personality of Madame Costes. It's her hotel, and you can tell. 'Costes' has become a brand name in Paris, synonymous with stylish surroundings and good food … and Karen Costes is part of the same dynasty, and Bourg Tibourg is no exception.

address Hôtel Bourg Tibourg, 19 rue du Bourg-Tibourg, 75004 Paris
tel (33) (0)1 42 78 47 39   **fax** (33) (0)1 40 29 07 00
e-mail hotel@bourgtibourg.com
room rates from €160

absolutely have to see
Hôtel de Ville, 29 rue de Rivoli, 75004 Paris (tel 01 42 76 43 43): a French Renaissance masterpiece that leaves other town halls looking rather drab

must have brunch
Mariage Frères, 30 rue du Bourg-Tibourg, 75004 Paris (tel 01 42 72 28 11): eccentrically memorable colonial-era tea room, where tea is the foundation of all the drinks and dishes on the menu; a true Marais original

caron de beaumarchais

Inventor, clockmaker, musician, playwright, raconteur, aristocrat, political activist: Caron de Beaumarchais was one of the most colourful characters of eighteenth-century Paris. First and foremost he was one of Louis XV's favourite clockmakers, a position and title that provided him with an apartment in the Louvre and access to the King's inner circle. He was also the author of *The Marriage of Figaro*. Yet despite his links to the upper echelons of Bourbon power, he managed to escape the fate of most Parisian bluebloods thanks to his active sponsorship of the American Revolution. The hundreds of guns that he sold to America at no profit earned him the timely respect of France's Revolutionary Council.

'Caron de Beaumarchais' is the perfect name for this small hotel, and not only because he used to live next door. It exemplifies a certain refined approach to life. I had walked past its immaculate blue-painted timber façade many times, assuming it to be a chic decorator's showroom or perhaps an antique shop. The tiny lobby features a rare pianoforte from 1792, a black marble Louis XV fireplace, an antique card table and a handful of gilded wall sconces and antique mirrors. That's a lot of detail and a lot of antique packed into a tiny space, and it typifies the formula proprietor Alain Bigeard has followed throughout his nineteen-room hotel. The ceiling of every guest room features twisted and mangled exposed oak beams. The furniture is Louis XVI (the simple and more elegant Gustavian variety), and the fabrics are from the venerable French textile houses Nobilis Fontan and Le Manach. The impression is authentically antique, just as one would hope to find in Paris.

There are also some very modern luxuries, including brand-new bathrooms. The entire building was dismantled, leaving only the eighteenth-century façade standing. All the beautiful old parts – like the ceiling beams and wrought-iron balustrade – were saved and installed in a completely new building that has elevators and up-to-date plumbing, wiring and telecommunications, including satellite TV. The effect is old, but the convenience is new.

If Caron de Beaumarchais sounds like the perfect Parisian hotel experience, that's because it is – and it's perfectly affordable. There's really only one problem: you won't get a room unless you book well in advance.

address Hôtel Caron de Beaumarchais, 12 rue Vieille du Temple, 75004 Paris
tel (33) (0)1 42 72 34 12 **fax** (33) (0)1 42 72 34 63
e-mail hotel@carondebeaumarchais.com
room rates from €125

absolutely have to see
Centre Pompidou, Place Georges Pompidou, 75004 Paris (tel 01 44 78 12 33): modern art housed in Richard Rogers and Renzo Piano's breathtakingly original 1970s 'inside-out' building

must have lunch
Georges in the Centre Pompidou (tel 01 44 78 47 99): stunning cutting-edge architecture of contoured aluminium inside, panoramic views of Paris outside

rive gauche

Rive Gauche: so chic that Yves Saint Laurent gave its name to a perfume.... The Left Bank of the Seine, comprising parts of the 5th, 6th and 7th arrondissements, represents everything people expect Paris to be. It has the bridges and quais, the quaint little streets packed with *antiquaires*, boutiques and romantic restaurants; it has Les Deux Magots, Café de Flore and Brasserie Lipp; and it has the shopping cachet of Boulevard Saint-Germain and the rue de Grenelle.

For culture vultures the area also features some of the most important museums in the city, including the Musée Rodin, the Musée d'Orsay and the Orangerie at the Jardin du Luxembourg. And, frankly, the Louvre isn't far away either, just a short stroll across the Pont Neuf.

It's no wonder, then, that dominant figures in the world of fashion – Hubert de Givenchy, Karl Lagerfeld, Sonia Rykiel and so on – choose to live here. Same goes for the prominent names of

French film – Catherine Deneuve and Roman Polanski, for example. How do I know this for certain? Because they all buy their *huitres* and *langoustines* from the same fishmonger on rue du Bac and their names are clearly written on the spines of their account books.

The Rive Gauche has long been a 'power' neighbourhood. Members of the political elite built their spectacular *hôtels particuliers* in the vicinity of the Assemblée Nationale (the lower house of the French parliament), which explains the density of extraordinary 18th- and 19th-century architectural gems hidden behind towering walls and imposing handsomely painted timber gates.

For the first-time visitor to Paris, the Left Bank is *the* place to be, because it fulfils all the expectations one has of this well-preserved city. It may be a cliché, but it's a cliché executed in the very best taste and style.

st thomas d'aquin

Of all the Highly Individual Places in Paris, the Saint Thomas d'Aquin is the one I'd be most tempted to keep to myself. Located on a quiet, idyllic street that runs between Boulevard Saint-Germain and rue de l'Université, it's everyone's idea of the perfect little Left Bank hotel.

Covered in ivy, with pale blue-grey shutters and lots of tiny balconies in wrought-iron filigree, this Parisian gem is regarded quite proprietorially by its guests. One American lady was horrified when she discovered I was photographing the hotel for this book. 'But,' she spluttered – as if to say 'this is my little secret, and I don't want to share it' – 'I've been staying here for more than two decades…. Just imagine, God forbid, next time I call I won't be able to get a room!'

The lady has a point. With room prices starting around 130 Euros, this engagingly chic bolthole is a real bargain. But now that I've announced it to all and sundry, you might well wonder how much longer this will last. The answer to that has a lot to do with the mindset of Bertrand Plasmans, the proprietor. Plasmans is quite aware that he could charge more for his establishment, but he genuinely seems to get a kick out of providing what one guest described to me as '*outrageous* value'.

The formula is deceptively simple: a slick, clean, contemporary interior behind a charming, old, stone-fronted façade. Designwise it's not the kind of place that has you gasping for superlatives, but it's all done in good taste even if nothing stands out as especially original or unique. And that's the way Plasmans wants it. The design might not be the topic at the next dinner party you go to, but neither will it be yesterday's news.

One thing is for certain: this is one of those rare places that looks much better in real life than in photographs. The hotel's stylish simplicity and handsome colour scheme seem to evade capture on film, but its real-life charm has not evaded its clientele.

Nor has its location. A mere stone's throw from the hotel are many examples of the kind of restaurant – small, intimate, romantic – that people come to Paris for, as well as some of the best antique shops in the world, and of course some of the most famous cafés. Even if you don't manage to venture more than a block in any direction for the duration of your stay, you won't be frustrated, so rich is this little area in fine things to do, see and eat.

address Hôtel Saint Thomas d'Aquin, 3 rue du Pré-aux-Clercs, 75007 Paris
tel (33) (0)1 42 61 01 22 **fax** (33) (0)1 42 61 41 43
e-mail hotelsaintthomasdaquin@wanadoo.fr
room rates from €130

absolutely have to see
The chi-chi boutiques along the rue de Grenelle

must have lunch
Le Procope, 13 rue de l'Ancienne Comédie, 75006 Paris (tel 01 40 46 79 00): join the intellectuals at what's reputed to be the oldest restaurant in Paris

l'hôtel

The plaque on the wall reads: 'Oscar Wilde died here in 1900.' Something tells you that this hotel, situated in the appropriately named rue des Beaux-Arts, was never going to fade into obscurity … which would no doubt have pleased the great wit Wilde, who, even on his deathbed, broke and broken, managed to quip, 'I am dying as I have lived: beyond my means.'

In fact L'Hôtel probably pioneered the notion of a small, highly creative, highly individual hotel. When I first stayed here in the early 1980s, each room was decorated to a funny individual theme and all the guest rooms opened onto an extraordinary, round, neoclassical stairwell, but the restaurant was virtually non-existent and everything was a bit rough around the edges. The architecture, however, and the location – almost next door to the entrance of the famous Ecole des Beaux-Arts – more than made up for it.

Then the new proprietor, Guy-Louis Duboucheron, set about renovating this precious Left Bank jewel. At his invitation Jacques Garcia, whose name in design is built on reverence for history, took up the transformation. The result is a *bonbonnière* of rich detail and evocative decoration. Everything looks as it may have done at the time Wilde was in residence (although, I suspect, a bit smarter), and this includes Wilde's former room, with some of his framed correspondence.

But the best part of the newly renovated L'Hôtel would have to be the *caves*. In a space that usually sees nothing more than storage of dusty wine bottles, Garcia has created a Roman-style bathing facility complete with swimming pool and elaborate relaxation spaces.

The famed neoclassical stairwell now looks more appropriate than it has ever done. Decorated with plaster medallions and rising from a star-patterned inlaid stone floor towards a dome that is open to the sky, this internal tower is truly magnificent. There is nothing like it in Paris, yet it is the kind of *folie* that is perfectly at home in an address on the rue des Beaux-Arts.

And, with a smidgeon of imagination, it is not hard to imagine Oscar Wilde holding court in a corner of Le Restaurant, the hotel's elegant dining room.

address L'Hôtel, 13 rue des Beaux-Arts, 75006 Paris
tel (33) (0)1 44 41 99 00 **fax** (33) (0)1 43 25 64 81
e-mail stay@l-hotel.com
room rates from €255

absolutely have to see
Ecole Nationale Supérieure des Beaux-Arts, 14 rue Bonaparte, 75006 Paris
(tel 01 47 03 50 00): without doubt the most impressive and most historic art
school in the world

must have lunch
Le Restaurant, the engaging restaurant on the ground floor of L'Hôtel,
marrying First and Second Empire with Belle Epoque

HOTEL
DE
TOURISME
-H-
MINISTÈRE
chargé du

SORTIE DE
SECOURS

PRIÈRE DE
NE PAS
STATIONNER
DEVANT
CETTE PORTE

duc de saint-simon

Not everyone who comes to Paris wants to stay at the Ritz. Yes, it's grand and colourful and Coco Chanel used to live there, but for many people the real Paris is summed up in a different way: intimate, charming, surprising, revealing itself only to those willing to walk along its multitude of little streets. The real fun is the way in which so much of the city's impressive beauty is hidden behind imposing *portes* and high stone walls. There's a magic to this architectural layering, and there are a handful of small hotels that share this slightly medieval appeal.

One enduring favourite is the Duc de Saint-Simon. Part of the secret of the hotel's attraction is that, like the city itself, it feels as if it's somehow hidden away. Tucked down a little side street, a stone's throw from the rue de Grenelle, one of the best shopping strips in the 7th arrondissement, the Duc is a romantic fantasy for people who like their Paris à la *Aristocats* – old-fashioned, genteel and decoratively decadent.

In what would once have been the space for turning a carriage around, the hotel has created a Mad Hatter's garden-party courtyard straight from *Alice in Wonderland*. It's frilly and very French, and that's exactly why no visitor walking past can ever resist taking a second look.

The interior – a mix of Belle Epoque, grand-style flea-market finds and faux finishes – looks as if it could have been the work of star decorator Jacques Garcia, but in fact it pre-dates Garcia by a decade or two, and in this case the Venetian mirrors, toile de Jouy, canopy beds, Louis XVI chairs, orientalist detailing and fancy secretaires were not part of a master plan; they were simply accumulated more in a manner one would find in one's own house.

Crystal chandeliers, boiserie, marble, cracked paint, tufted this, glazed that: the Duc is a one-stop shop for French decorative arts, softened by the fact that it's a bit faded and dog-eared by the passage of time. There are no grand staircases to swish down, or exotic spas to indulge in; no trendy bars, no Roman-style swimming pool, no polished-brass-button uniforms … just a discreetly tasteful classic address in Paris that puts the best of the Left Bank – the Musée Rodin, the Musée d'Orsay, Café de Flore, Les Deux Magots, Brasserie Lipp, Ladurée and the fabulous shopping of Boulevard Saint-Germain and the rue de Grenelle – within easy walking distance.

address Hôtel Duc de Saint-Simon, 14 rue de Saint-Simon, 75007 Paris
tel (33) (0)1 44 39 20 20 **fax** (33) (0)1 45 48 68 25
e-mail duc.de.saint.simon@wanadoo.fr
room rates from €245

absolutely have to see
Musée Rodin, 77 rue de Varenne, 75007 Paris (tel 01 44 18 61 10): recently refurbished masterpiece of 18th-century palace and elaborate garden chock-a-block with Rodin's most famous works

must have lunch
The café in the garden of the Musée Rodin, April–October: the food is simple, but eating surrounded by Rodin's sculpture makes it memorable

hôtel verneuil

Finding the hotel that defies being found must be one of the enduring pleasures of Paris – partly because it's never easy, mainly because the reward is a bit like finding a famous restaurant that just happens to have a free table.

Verneuil must rank as one of the most elusive of all hotels. Perfectly positioned on tiny rue de Verneuil, a street with more than its fair share of antique dealers and exotic little restaurants, the hotel blends so successfully into its surroundings that I must have walked past it dozens of times without realizing it was a hotel. My son's nursery school was across the street, and still I hadn't noticed it. Not that the building gives much away: there's a small sign, I think, but the ground-floor interior could just as easily be a rare book dealer's salon or a decorator's office.

All of which, of course, enhances the delight of finally stumbling through the front door and claiming your prize: a room. Yellow, pink, baby blue, absinthe green: at Verneuil the rooms come in all the colours you would almost predict a cute little hotel on the Left Bank to have. Needless to say, the decor of each room is completely different and, if you're one of the first guests to arrive, the staff sometimes take you up and down the spiral stairs to find your favourite.

Apart from breakfast, and perhaps a drink by the fire in the cosy salon after 6 o'clock, there's not much on offer in the hotel itself – and that suits most of the guests perfectly. Particularly in this part of Paris there's so much to see and do and eat that hanging around the hotel would be to waste valuable hedonist time.

The point of Hôtel Verneuil is that it forces you to get out and make the most of the Rive Gauche. Between them, the nearby rue des Saints-Pères and rue de l'Université, as well as rue de Verneuil itself, probably house the best and most diverse antique shops in the world; every other café in the area is an institution or a famous landmark; and in between are the small hidden restaurants and completely original boutiques that make this part of Paris such a magnet for people with a penchant for one-off individuality and a persuasive sense of style. In other words, stay in your hotel room and you've missed the point.

And, just as importantly, with the money you save on the hotel you can buy yourself some champagne at Ladurée.

address Hôtel Verneuil, 8 rue de Verneuil, 75007 Paris
tel (33) (0)1 42 60 82 14 **fax** (33) (0)1 42 61 40 38
e-mail info@hotelverneuil.com
room rates from €130

absolutely have to see
Musée d'Orsay, 1 rue de la Légion d'Honneur, 75007 Paris (tel 01 40 49 48 14): former train station converted into museum of 19th-century fine arts (don't miss the Impressionist wing)

must have lunch
Ladurée, 21 rue Bonaparte, 75006 Paris (tel 01 44 07 64 87): Belle Epoque-style café and restaurant, famous for its macaroons

montalembert

When it first opened in the late 1980s, the Montalembert marked the arrival of a completely new type of city hotel. Smaller, slicker and more sophisticated, it was a hotel for the style-conscious traveller.

In a strange way, the hotel blossomed as much by what it didn't do as by what it did. It didn't have the fancy uniforms, the ballroom or the garage-size reception area, nor did it have a shopping arcade, numerous bars or a variety of restaurants. It had no presidential suite and no Olympic-sized swimming pool in Augustus Caesar-styled spa. Yet a room didn't cost that much less than one at the Ritz. Guests, however, knew exactly what they were paying for....

They were paying for the contemporary luxury of Christian Liaigre's design; for the pleasure of a room evoking calm and serenity; for the charm of a bijou restaurant with plenty of ambience but very little fuss. The Montalembert was modern and stylish, and guests couldn't get enough of it. The hotel was a hit from the go-get. It connected with grown-up travellers in a grown-up way. And it substantiated hotelier Grace Leo-Andrieu's conviction that quality doesn't have to come in grand packages to be convincing.

Almost two decades later Leo-Andrieu has moved on to other projects and the chic, but preferably not too large, city hotel has become an established genre. But despite Leo-Andrieu's departure, and the fact that much of Liaigre's original work has been updated and redone, the Montalembert continues to deliver the goods, attracting travellers who do not wish to compromise on taste or privacy.

The adjective that springs to mind for the Montalembert is 'mellow'. The hotel has mellowed, and for hotels as well as for whiskies, this is a good thing.

The location does it no harm either. Situated on rue de Montalembert, it's only steps away from rue du Bac, possibly the most enchanting street on the Left Bank. Some of the best and most original shopping in Paris can be done on 'Bac', as it's known. The famous antiquarians are in the immediate neighbourhood and the area is crisscrossed with funky little cafés and restaurants, the best in Paris being just next door.

address Hôtel Montalembert, 3 rue de Montalembert, 75007 Paris
tel (33) (0)1 45 49 68 68/01/02   **fax** (33) (0)1 45 49 69 49
e-mail welcome@montalembert.com
room rates from €350

absolutely have to see
The eclectic shops on the rue du Bac

must have lunch
L'Atelier de Joël Robuchon, 7 rue de Montalembert, 75007 Paris (tel 01 42 22 56 56): a culinary voyage and adventure with a 3-Michelin-star chef

bel ami

'The hotel … faced the St Germain des Prés. On Sundays we sat at the Deux Magots and watched the people…. There were long conversations about the ballet over sauerkraut in Lipp and blank recuperative hours over books and prints in rue Bonaparte.' So wrote Zelda Fitzgerald in 1924.

I found this passage in a book of collected writings relating to Paris, and in its casual, elegant simplicity it sums up the pleasure of one of the city's most alluring and enduring attractions: doing nothing in great style, at no particular speed. I can't think of any other city that makes being idle such a pleasant and rewarding experience. What's more, Fitzgerald's version of Paris hasn't dated at all. You can still sit at Deux Magots and watch the people; you can still order the sauerkraut at Brasserie Lipp; and you can still browse endlessly through the nearby book-shops.

As Joseph Barry put it, 'The bedrock Parisian trait is resistance to change.' When Parisians do change, they manage to do it in a way that harmonizes seamlessly with the things they leave unchanged. Thus you can enjoy the cutting-edge contemporaneity of Hôtel Bel Ami, with its dark timber veneers, signature clean white lines and soft sensuous shapes, then walk out the door, head a hundred yards up the road and engage in the same café life – indeed, in the same café – as Hemingway, Picasso, Henry James, F. Scott Fitzgerald and co.

For location alone, Bel Ami would never be short on customers, but its chic modernity adds another dimension to one of Paris's most attractive areas, so why settle for one world when you can straddle two?

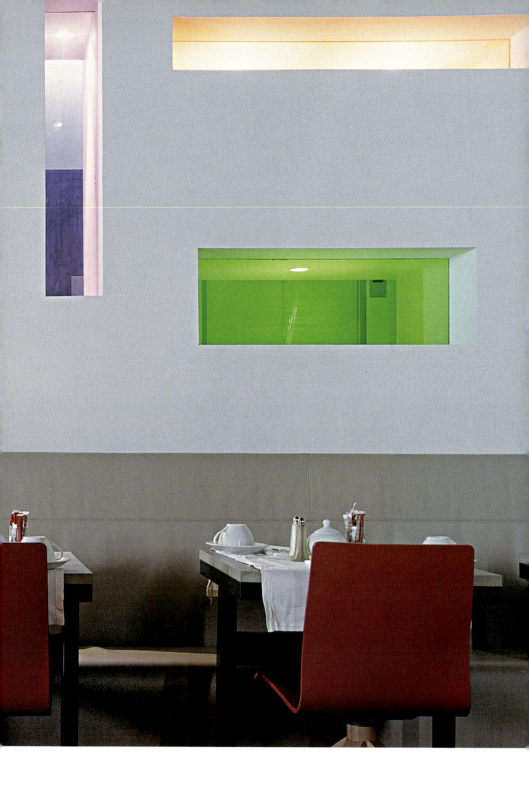

Better still, when the Bel Ami first opened in January 2000, there was a newness to it that was a little stark. There was also the fact that the restaurant, located in a basement, replaced a slightly down-at-heel jazz joint. Pretty much anyone who could remember the jazz club would have concurred that they should have kept it. But now that the restaurant has moved to a light-filled space on the ground floor, and now that the hotel is flanked by two proper, smoke-filled, late-night jazz caverns, everything is as it should be – perfectly Rive Gauche.

address Hôtel Bel Ami, 7–11 rue St Benoît, 75006 Paris
tel (33) (0)1 42 61 53 53   **fax** (33) (0)1 49 27 09 33
e-mail contact@hotel-bel-ami.com
room rates from €270

absolutely have to see
Jardin Luxembourg, the most beautiful park in Paris, and the Orangerie,
a popular venue for record-setting exhibitions of the likes of Gauguin

must have lunch
The café at Emporio Armani, 149 Boulevard Saint-Germain, 75006 Paris
(tel 01 53 63 33 50): the best Italian restaurant on the Left Bank … and
the best-kept secret

le triangle d'or

People who know Paris will tell you, in a resigned tone of voice, that the Champs-Elysées is no longer what it was. Ruined by the likes of McDonald's, Virgin megastores and Disney emporiums, it's a grand boulevard with not so grand tenants. But then London's Oxford Street and New York's Fifth Avenue aren't as glamorous as they used to be either.

In truth, the elegantly expensive boutiques, the charming cafés and the special little places for lunch that typify the chic of the 8th are still to be found in the Golden Triangle. Just one street over from the Champs-Elysées are streets such as rue François 1er, chock-a-block with trendy bars, chi-chi shops, fashionable restaurants and – since recently – hip hotels; very hip hotels.

Designed by the elite of French decorating hierarchy, these are venues that resonate with interesting and fanciful history. This is the Paris of Audrey Hepburn, in which shopping, lunch,

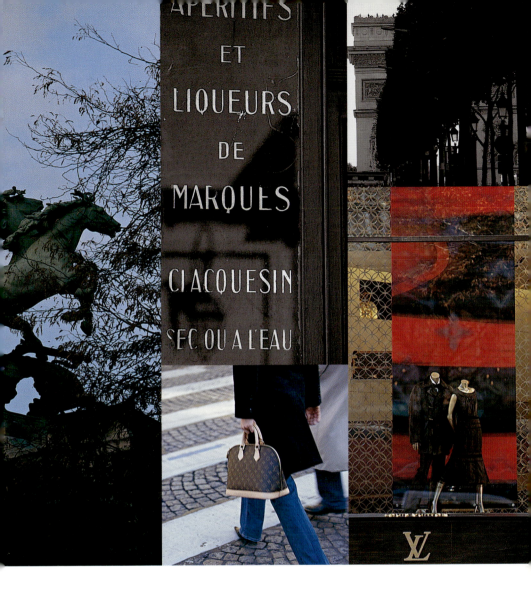

more shopping, spa and dinner constitute the perfect day. Some people call the area old-fashioned, and they are right if they're referring to the service. In this neighbourhood it would be unthinkable for your apéritif to arrive *sans* olives.

People in the 8th seem to be engaged in a permanent, and ultimately successful, battle to be as elegantly turned out as their surroundings. Walking on the street without a jacket would be like having a one-course lunch....

Because it's newer, the area is not as well endowed with monumental legacies as the 1st, which is fine, because if it were you wouldn't have time for the other pursuits the neighbourhood has to offer. This is Paris for hedonists. It isn't cheap but it is unique. Nowhere in the world will you find such a density of perfectly refined establishments catering to grown-up pleasure.

de sers

At the turn of the century, France was in the bloom of Napoleon III's Second Empire, Baron Haussmann had completed his grand remodelling of Paris, and the 8th arrondissement had become the aristocracy's neighbourhood of choice, symbolizing as it did the Belle Epoque's elegance and style. So it was that in 1880 Henri-Léopold Charles, the Marquis de Sers, purchased a plot of land a stone's throw from the Champs-Elysées and commissioned architect Jules Pellichet to create a classic, luxurious *hôtel particulier*.

Parisian townhouses of this period shared certain characteristics: they all needed a *porte cochère* (a covered gangway that would enable Monsieur and Madame to alight from their carriage without getting wet), a courtyard in which to turn the carriage around, stables for the horses, a grand staircase of course, and a *piano nobile*, or first floor with grand rooms for entertaining. How many of these original features remain today varies from building to building. In the case of the Marquis de Sers's house, it had lost most of its architectural identity due to a century of alterations and additions, and was almost unrecognizable by the time proprietor Thibault Vidalenc and architect Thomas Vidalenc (they are cousins) commenced the gargantuan task of giving it a new lease of life. Fortunately the Vidalencs recognized that its beauty, grace and true history rested with its origins as a private mansion.

The easy way out would have been for Thibault simply to redecorate, but instead the hybrid building was torn apart and the original spaces re-excavated. When it came to decorating and furnishing, the pair rejected the historical model in favour of a more eclectic one.

Architect Thomas, a self-confessed traveller, relied on his own experience with hotels across the world to avoid, as he puts it, 'the old-fashioned drapes and fake-Louis furniture approach' of grand hotels. Instead he chose to focus on the quality of the space. As such, the furniture, particularly in the guest rooms, is as unobtrusive and modern as possible, yet he was also inspired by his travels to incorporate a simple sense of culture.

The result is very much true to the Vidalencs' plans to evoke the spirit of the once-aristocratic home. The building has recovered the charisma of a Belle Epoque mansion, the guest rooms are convincing in their spaciousness, and the presence of a scattered collection of traditional oil portraits in ornate gilded frames adds a decorative swish to the contemporary interior. What *les cousins* will not tell you is what a stylish, modern and original hotel they've created. For that they're far too old-fashioned....

address Hôtel de Sers, 41 ave Pierre 1er de Serbie, 75008 Paris
tel (33) (0)1 53 23 75 75 **fax** (33) (0)1 53 23 75 76
e-mail contact@hoteldesers.com
room rates from €450

absolutely have to see
The newly renovated Petit Palais (tel 01 53 43 40 00) and Grand Palais
(tel 01 44 13 17 30), avenue Winston Churchill, 75008 Paris: Napoleon III's
fabulous glass-topped wedding cakes housing temporary exhibitions

must have dinner
Bound, 49–51 avenue George V, 75008 Paris (tel 01 53 67 84 60):
the most *branché* (cool) bar and restaurant in the 8th

pershing hall

A few years ago I was invited by some property developers to look at a hotel project they had just commenced in the chi-chi 8th arrondissement. It was a rather grand *hôtel particulier* that had belonged to an equally grand four-star American soldier – General Pershing. Without a doubt the property had great potential, and the fact that French superstar designer Andrée Putman was on board gave it further cachet. But the thing that intrigued and distracted me most was the subtle – not usually a word associated with American generals – integration of US army imagery into the French decorative detail.

Louis XV-style wrought-iron railings with recurring military stars; carved stone busts, not of famous French historical figures but of anonymous army, navy and airforce recruits … a game of spot-the-military-reference. The closer you looked, the more evidence you found that the owner of this house loved the army and France in equal measure, and that he had a sense of humour as well as a sense of style.

To the developers' credit, all the Pershing bits are still here, which distinguishes this former aristocratic home from other French aristocratic inner-city mansions. Nonetheless General Pershing would undoubtedly be amazed at what has become of his former townhouse.

Designwise, Putman's masterstroke was to convert the courtyard into a restaurant – open in summer, covered in winter – with a vertical garden. Trees, bushes, long grasses and other plants grow up a specially treated four-storey-high wall that provides the focal point for the dining crowd. What's more, all the other public spaces have been designed just as cleverly.

The ballroom, the downstairs lounge, the terrace bar and the main bar with its chic mezzanine level all look into the central courtyard space, providing a focus for the entire hotel which has nothing to do with anything happening out on the street. It's the kind of privacy most hotels dream about; an environment – and a very stylish one at that – which is completely unaffected by outside traffic or noise.

With its hot bar, fashionable restaurant and stylish, clean-cut guest rooms, Pershing Hall is a place of which the general would no doubt approve, and he would also no doubt appreciate the design discipline applied to his old HQ. As for political correctness, a hip hotel is surely a more desirable legacy than a weapon of mass destruction.

address Pershing Hall, 49 rue Pierre Charron, 75008 Paris
tel (33) (0)1 58 36 58 00 **fax** (33) (0)1 58 36 58 01
e-mail info@pershinghall.com
room rates from €420

absolutely have to see
The high-end shops on the avenue de Montaigne

must have lunch
The hotel restaurant in the courtyard downstairs (on a sunny day, if possible)

lancaster

After reinventing the small Left Bank hotel with the Montalembert in the 7th, Grace Leo-Andrieu launched into redefining luxury on the Right Bank, in the chi-chi Triangle d'Or, no less.

How does one compete with the likes of the Crillon, the Ritz and the Meurice? The answer, for Leo-Andrieu, was in two words: 'privacy' and 'personality'.

Paris has a strong tradition of safeguarding the privacy of well-known clients. These guests, in turn, have made a historic habit of personalizing their hotel spaces: Coco Chanel, for example, had a suite at the Ritz, and Marlene Dietrich kept an apartment at the Lancaster in its 1930s heyday. This tradition proved the inspiration and cornerstone for Leo-Andrieu's second Paris hotel. She would provide privacy for her guests (celebrities or otherwise) and she would create lots of spaces with different personalities. Thus, from the building blocks of discretion and individuality, Leo-Andrieu created a hotel where all the rooms – and in particular the suites – vary in decorative style as well as in shape and layout. As might be expected, guests have grown accustomed to their particular favourites, and this gives the hotel a familiar, almost clubbish feel.

Designwise, Leo-Andrieu opted for a contemporary approach similar to the Montalembert's, but with one difference: when she and her husband, property developer Stéphane Andrieu, purchased the hotel it was chock-full of antiques (the previous owner, it seemed, was a lifelong devotee of the *puces*, Paris's extraordinary flea markets). All these treasures were duly cleaned, repaired or restored and then placed back into a more modern, less fussy interior.

This eclectic combination of contemporary and antique, with a twist of Chinoiserie, is what defines the style of the Lancaster: a Louis XV clock, a modern sofa, a Louis XVI desk, a slick and streamlined bathroom panelled in big slabs of Carrera marble....

Attracted by its unique style and its reputation for discretion, many famous names have made the Lancaster their favourite, but the hotel is, of course, far too discreet to name names.

address Hôtel Lancaster, 7 rue de Berri, Champs-Elysées, 75008 Paris
tel (33) (0)1 40 76 40 76 **fax** (33) (0)1 40 76 40 00
e-mail reservations@hotel-lancaster.fr
room rates from €470

absolutely have to see
Paris from the top of the Arc de Triomphe: walk out of the hotel and up the Champs-Elysées and then up the stairs (you'll be one up on Napoleon: he died before it was finished)

must have lunch
The hotel restaurant: culinary landmark in the 8th with extraordinary courtyard garden, contemporary Chinoiserie decor and cuisine by Michel Troisgros

le a

Look at any list of top-ranking restaurants in Paris and you will notice that more than a fair share of them are in the 8th arrondissement. In fact, most of them are in the 8th. No wonder, then, that this Golden Triangle also has so much variety on offer in terms of hotels.

The 8th has an almost limitless appetite for luxury – not necessarily the gold taps and leopardskin variety but the brand of luxury that the French are such masters at: subtle, discreet, using only the best materials … luxury that *suggests* wealth and privilege rather than screams it.

Given this appetite for quality and refinement, it is understandable that the owner of Le A wanted to create a hotel with Frédéric Méchiche. A designer on the same level as Andrée Putman, Jacques Garcia and Christian Liaigre, in terms of diversity of work and desirable list of high-profile clients, Méchiche was already well known for his conversion of Dokhan's into a *des res* in the 16th. But Le A is hardly a copy of the same in a different arrondissement.

Le A is New Méchiche. Gone are the layers of neoclassical reference, the boiserie, the gilded frames, the Adam-style symmetry, the rich velvets, the decorative copper nails, the signature striped cotton ticking applied to walls and repro Louis furniture. What is left is his enduring ability to make small spaces seem immense and his enviable talent for a soft kind of minimalism: soft as in welcoming, cosy even, without sacrificing the edge of all that white. His stripes are still there, but pared down and muted. What is not muted is the art. At Le A the art and the design are, for once, on a par. Which is how it should be.

Méchiche worked closely with the artist Fabrice Hybert and every space, from the lounge areas to the guest rooms and even the hallway on the ground floor, has been transformed into an installation. It's a sophisticated approach that chimes with a certain clientele. Not all guests are familiar with the artist's work when they arrive, but one thing is certain: they will be when they leave. Not that the art is difficult to live with. Quite the contrary. But by making use of art and by paring down the interior (space is significantly enhanced by clever use of mirrors and there is a distinctly soothing lack of clutter), the rooms are refreshingly liberating and evince a serenity of composure. Art-speak as this may sound, it works....

As for Méchiche, Le A seems to be a true representation of his current work and sensibilities, and in the 8th such distinction is much appreciated (and very well slept in).

address Hôtel Le A, 4 rue d'Artois, 75008 Paris
tel (33) (0)1 42 56 99 99 **fax** (33) (0)1 42 56 99 90
e-mail hotel-le-a@wanadoo.fr
room rates from €329

absolutely have to see
The boutiques and antique shops off nearby rue Faubourg Saint-Honoré

must have dinner
Market, 15 avenue Matignon, 75008 Paris (tel 01 56 43 40 90): Jean-Georges Vongerichten's triumphant return in a restaurant designed by Christian Liaigre

'HIVER

11th arrondissement

Parisians who draw, paint, act, direct, write, etc. will tell you that the 11th is the new 3rd. To non-Parisians this may sound like numerical mumbo-jumbo, but in fact it's really no different from what happens in all big cities – the gentrification of one area and the emergence of another.

In Paris, the 11th is where you go if your own story is 'more dash than cash'. Interesting shops, bars and restaurants are popping up, due largely to the fact that the proprietors can afford the rent, but also because the audience is younger and less 'bourgeois'. The residential mantra is loft-living: there aren't many apartment buildings with concierge, sweeping staircase and birdcage elevator. But what the area lacks in sumptuous grandness it makes up for in street cred. People love the fact that the Gare du Nord and Gare de Lyon are close by, that the Canal Saint-Martin is still intact, and that the population is far more multicultural than, say, in the 16th.

A new kind of Paris is emerging from the 11th, and that's a good thing, because without edgier neighbourhoods like this, the city would stagnate into a tasteful assortment of high-class museums and elegant stores – beautiful, definitely, but without any vibrancy or soul. And that wouldn't be right, especially for the arrondissement that houses the very heart of French democratic principles, the Place de la République. Built by Baron Haussmann and dominated by Léopold and Charles Morice's 1883 statue symbolizing the French Republic, this square is one of the bustling hubs of the city.

In a sense, you can get the best of both worlds in the 11th because it borders on the 3rd, i.e. the Marais is right next door. So you can go 'chic and sophisticated' or 'street and real'. *Liberté, égalité, fraternité*: the choice is yours.

le general

Tucked just behind the Place de la République, on quiet rue Rampon, on the very eastern border of the Marais, Le General introduces affordable, contemporary style to the 11th.

And for once this style is not limited to the first twelve or so people lucky enough to get a room. With 47 rooms, Le General offers something new – affordability on a larger scale. In other words, when you call last minute, having decided to spend a long weekend in Paris without any planning, there's every chance you'll get a room.

And the rooms offer something that is also in rather short supply in Paris, namely space and light. In designing the interiors, architect Jean-Philippe Nuel opted for an approach that forsakes decorative detail in favour of, in his words, 'warm modernity'. For those of us who prefer a world without soundbites, this means white walls, white bathrooms, off-white curtains, rosewood and ash-coloured timber, flatscreen TVs and the odd splash of colour in a red zebra-print chair or purple Starck-designed plastic stool. In short, nothing that you won't have seen before, but that's fine because it was not Nuel's intent to be experimental. Simply by providing spacious rooms with clean lines, plenty of natural light and contemporary decor, it is by Parisian standards plenty different.

The other pragmatic side of Le General's scale is the services it provides. The reception is open 24 hours, which, if you've ever stood outside a decidedly locked hotel at 3 a.m. on a winter's morning trying to remember where you put that piece of paper with the door code, is a tangible plus. And there's a real gym and sauna and massage room in the fitness centre.

On the food front, the hotel has no restaurant except for breakfast, but in this part of Paris that is decidedly not a problem. One side of the rue du Temple is the beginning of the Marais, where the choice is bewilderingly exotic, and in the other direction you quickly hit the Canal Saint-Martin and another part of Paris dense with cool cafés and characterful brasseries. All of which, combined with Le General itself, adds up to a formula that is not in the least stressful – and for that a lot of visitors to Paris are prepared to pay a lot.

address Le General Hotel, 5–7 rue Rampon, 75011 Paris
tel (33) (0)1 47 00 41 57 **fax** (33) (0)1 47 00 21 56
e-mail info@legeneralhotel.com
room rates from €135

absolutely have to see
Cirque d'Hiver Bouglione, 110 rue Amelot, 75011 Paris (tel 01 47 00 12 25): roll up for a truly spectacular Winter Circus

must have lunch
Le Clown Bar, 114 rue Amelot, 75011 Paris (tel 01 43 55 87 35): tiny atmospheric café plastered with vintage circus posters and with an original painted ceiling depicting clowns (the café is next door to the Cirque d'Hiver)

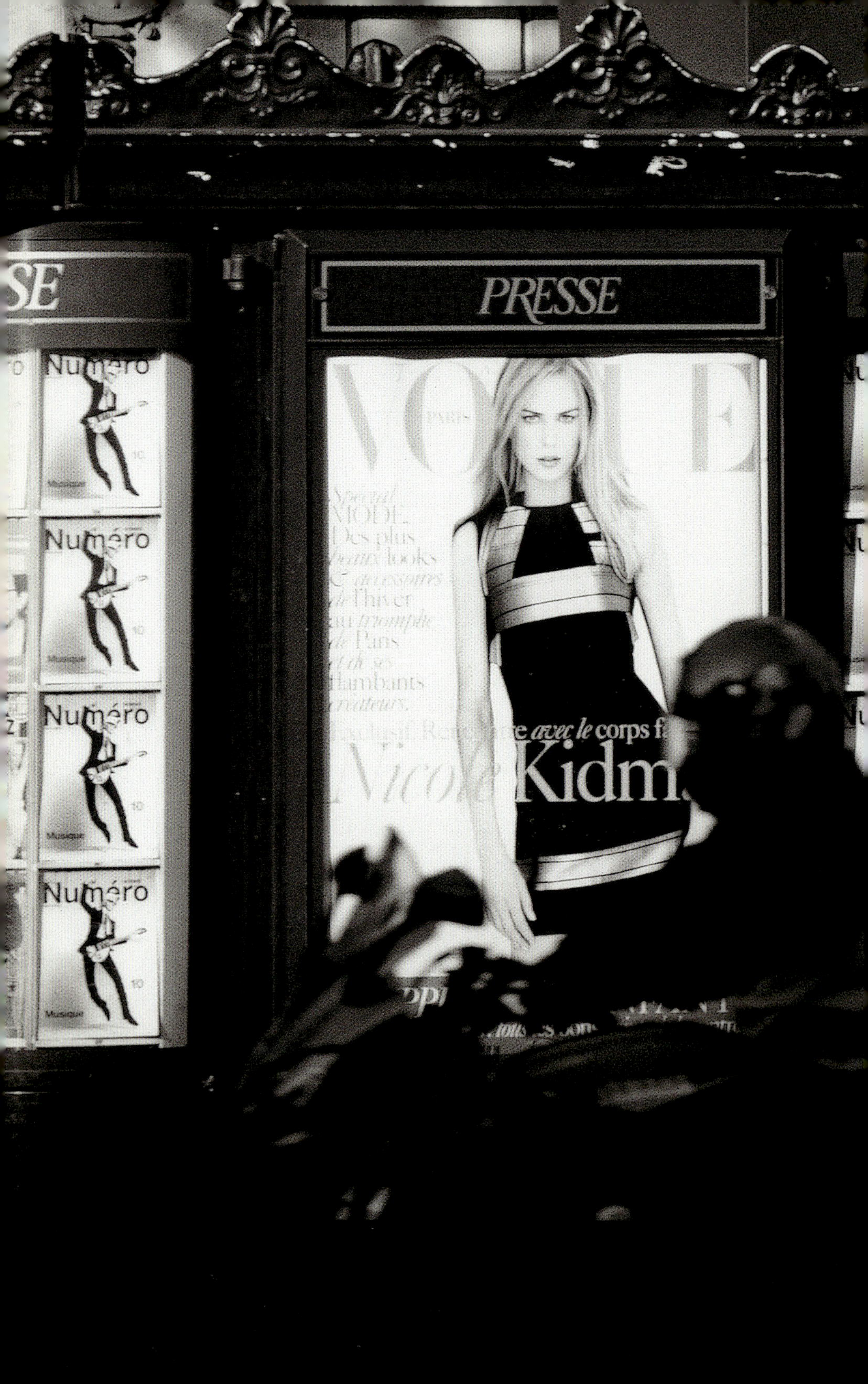

"Pour ne plus rame
ils ont décidé de nager

Paris is unique in that it's organized in the shape of a snail. Parisians think this is the most normal thing in the world; the rest of us find it admirably eccentric. The city does, however, in its organic spiral-shaped madness produce some interesting areas. The 13th is a good example. It borders the 5th, the 14th (Montparnasse) and the 6th, and as such it shares access without the prohibitively high real-estate prices. The 13th is favoured by students because it is still affordable and because of its close proximity to the schools and universities located in the 5th and 6th.

It's also known as Les Gobelins because this is the area that was mandated by Louis XIV for the manufacture of Gobelins tapestries. At the time a tapestry was the most prestigious product a person could own – like a Picasso or a Henry Moore, but even more exclusive – so the location became instantly historical, and has remained so ever since.

Apart from the Sun King's workshops, it's not an area with a huge number of monuments or museums, and it's different from the rest of Paris in that a large slice of it is taken up by Chinatown. Many visitors to Paris are surprised that the city even has a Chinatown, and that it goes on for kilometres. Actually it's said to be the biggest Chinatown in Europe: 'Hong Kong sur Seine'.

It's fun to see the interaction of French and Chinese cultures – neither known for their flexibility or love of change. But more importantly it's areas like Chinatown that make a city an interesting place to be. In this part of Paris you have no idea what to expect. The best way to discover it is on foot or by bicycle.

Cities need edge … and the 13th has got it.

la manufacture

La Manufacture is located just off Avenue des Gobelins, the name that first entered the French vocabulary when Louis XIV designated it as the new location of Les Manufactures Royales. Colbert, the King's chief minister, shifted all of Paris's weavers to this one location so they could create tapestries of the same dazzling magnitude as the Sun King's ego.

Aside from the workshops, this historic neighbourhood has been home to bohemian writers and the odd student rebellion. Great French thinkers like Voltaire, Hugo and Zola are buried in the nearby Pantheon and the Jardin des Plantes is virtually next door. These botanical gardens, established in 1626, are an excellent park and they also house a natural history museum and a zoo. To get a taste of the real Paris in this area, you just need to wander down the hill from the Pantheon and turn into the picturesque rue Mouffetard. One of the oldest streets in Paris, dating back to Roman times, it is full of small shops, open-air markets and affordable restaurants. The neighbourhood is also personalized by the academic focus of the Sorbonne, the city's oldest university. What is so good about this area is that it is beautiful, historic and fascinating without ever being pretentious.

The exterior of La Manufacture is pure nineteenth-century Haussmann: a grand five-storey limestone building with beautifully detailed wrought-iron balconies and relief carving to accentuate the classically proportioned doors and windows. Inside it's a different story – not quite minimalist but certainly contemporary and restrained. The pristine white walls are interrupted only by the vivid colour and geometry of paintings by local artist Alberto Cont.

Long before they thought about the interior design, the three-woman consortium of proprietors subjected the building to a thorough renovation that involved knocking down walls and installing an elevator, air conditioning and new plumbing (i.e. new bathrooms) throughout.

Oak floorboards, wicker chairs, cotton rugs, wooden furniture: these ingredients define a style that is both soft and natural. What could possibly be better than an affordable, attractive, well-situated hotel in Paris? That's easy. One that doesn't look affordable.

address Hôtel La Manufacture, 8 rue Philippe de Champagne, 75013 Paris
tel (33) (0)1 45 35 45 25   **fax** (33) (0)1 45 35 45 40
e-mail lamanufacture.paris@wanadoo.fr
room rates from €145

absolutely have to see
Fondation Cartier, 261 boulevard Raspail, 75014 Paris (tel 01 42 18 56 50): a glass-curtained exhibition centre that specializes in the more daring end of the scale

must have dinner
Le Polidor, 41 rue Monsieur Le Prince, 75006 Paris (tel 01 43 26 95 34): typical 'vieux Paris' restaurant, with crowded tables and simple good food

16th arrondissement

If there's one thing my father had an aversion to, it was being a tourist. That's probably why the 16th was his favourite arrondissement. He could do all the things he loved about Paris – sit in a café, enjoy a 'who cares about the cholesterol' lunch, drink a decent bottle of wine, shop for his favourite shirts at a classic little boutique, for his shoes at another – without anyone suspecting him to be anything but a Parisian. And why should they? Sure, there are a few expats living in the 16th, and there's the odd tour bus around Trocadéro, but that's about all.

For the most part the 16th is residential Paris at its purest. As might be expected, this arrondissement favours *boulangers*, boutiques and restaurants over museums and public spaces. Together with the 8th and the Left Bank, the 16th hosts a disproportionate number of highly rated restaurants. From La Grande Cascade, the former private lodge of Napoleon III in the

heart of the Bois de Boulogne to Prunier, an intact Art Deco monument of a restaurant on Avenue Victor Hugo, to the newly opened Crystal Room of Baccarat, Philippe Starck's extraordinary re-invention of the former mansion of Viscountess Marie-Laure de Noailles, the residents of the 16th are spoiled for choice.

But, you may say, there's more to life than eating and sitting in cafés. Indeed, do not be misled that all this patrician good living has overshadowed the city's lust for monumentality. There is plenty to see and admire in the 16th, the main thing being that it is of the more recent variety, i.e. the past 110 years. Art Nouveau, Art Deco and modernism are the creative signatures. Apart from obvious sites like Trocadéro and the Palais de Tokyo, there is, for instance, the Fondation Le Corbusier, a chance to wander round one of the architect's most successful houses.

dokhan's

This handsome, wedge-shaped, nineteenth-century, limestone building is in one of the most chic areas of Paris. Close to the famous Art Deco Trocadéro, with its fantastic view over the Eiffel Tower, the neighbourhood is full of elegant little restaurants and discreet boutiques.

It's an atmosphere and lifestyle into which Dokhan's blends perfectly. The designer responsible was Frédéric Méchiche. Like Jacques Garcia, Méchiche made his name creating private interiors for high-profile, big-name Parisians, and that is what made him such an inspired choice for this hotel. What Méchiche has given Dokhan's above all is a seductive mood – precisely the kind of mood people expect from Paris.

Take the hotel's champagne bar, for example. It is entirely panelled in exquisite eighteenth-century boiserie – wood panelling that was rescued by Méchiche, retailored to fit the space and painted a most unusual shade of chartreuse green with fine gilded detailing. The result is a space of remarkable character and quality, despite being relatively small. The champagne comes each week from a different vineyard and the food menu is designed to complement it, with simple dishes like cold salmon and potato.

What is so convincing in the design of Dokhan's is the overall impression of authenticity: the Adam-inspired neoclassical salon, the elegantly panelled reception, the old oak parquet floor, the massive doors, the velvet curtains and black-and-white tiled lobby. It's hard to believe that everything was stripped to the bare bones and created from scratch; that the entire ensemble here was conceived in Méchiche's imagination.

The most extraordinary guest spaces are on the top floor. There are four suites that make great use of the gabled and angled attics that are so typical of Paris. Each has its own unique personality. The Ming Suite, for example, is decorated entirely in the blue shades of Chinese porcelain. Another suite, the Eiffel, is a duplex in tones of beige, gold and black, with a small living room that has an unimpeded view of the Eiffel Tower. And this surprise and intimacy is not reserved to the suites. Because of the building's odd shape, it was possible to create an array of unusual spaces, each with the style and ambience unique to the designer.

address Sofitel Hôtel Trocadéro Dokhan's, 117 rue Lauriston, 75016 Paris
tel (33) (0)1 53 65 66 99 **fax** (33) (0)1 53 65 66 88
e-mail reservation@dokhans.com
room rates from €440

absolutely have to see
Trocadéro at night: there is no better time or place to view the spectacle of the Eiffel Tower in full glow

must have lunch
Tokyo Eat, Palais de Tokyo, 13 avenue du Président Wilson, 75016 Paris (tel 01 47 20 00 29): hangout housed in an exhibition space for modern art; Art Deco magnificence meets beatnik hip

sezz

The hotel's name is a play on its location. The 16th arrondisse- ment – or 'seizième', or 'sezz', as it's often referred to by the fast-talking Parisians who abbreviate almost everything – is the Parisian equivalent of New York's Upper East Side. This is where you'll find the most poodles and the most fur coats, but no facto- ries or offices, and no shortage of immaculately groomed, perfectly behaved children.

It's the part of Paris closest to the leafy Bois de Boulogne and it's the easiest location from which to escape to the country. It's also the cleanest, quietest, best manicured part of the city, and thus it ranks as the most desirable address for well-to-do Parisian families.

To be honest, it's the last arrondissement you would expect to find a hotel like Sezz. Designed by Christophe Pillet, a former protégé of Philippe Starck and a much sought-after designer of cutting-edge contemporary furniture, it's the kind of place you'd expect to find in the funky Marais ... which is exactly why its proprietor put it in the 16th.

Shahé Kalaidjian is an articulate, opinionated, Armenian, British, Lebanese hotelier, who thrives on going against the grain. 'Everyone', he will tell you, 'wants to be in the 16th, even if they won't admit it, not only because it's elegant and chic and refined but because it's 99.9% French.' And he's right. The 16th is a part of Paris that caters not to tourists but to Parisians. Prices are not inflated and the restaurants, cafés, brasseries and pharmacies (there's one on every corner) are of a very high standard because real Parisians are notoriously demanding.

The hotel's location gives it an edge, and its design breaks away from the tiny, suffering-for-art-in-the-attic type of establishment more usual in the area. Instead the Sezz gives the visitor the alternative option of space and art, big rooms with open-plan bathrooms, and beds that for once do not rest against a wall.

With Christophe Pillet, Shahé Kalaidjian got what he wanted, and more. It's not easy in a place like Paris to be different and stylish enough to get noticed, but they pulled it off. Even the traditional hotel bar got the treatment. Instead of some naff mini-pub that nobody ever used, or an honesty bar that only proves how dishonest people can be, Kalaidjian launched a genuinely new concept with champagne house Veuve Clicquot. The idea is simple: a bar that serves vintage Veuve by the glass – a chance to sample one of France's true luxuries at a fraction of what it would cost to buy a bottle. Try doing that at the Ritz....

address Hôtel Sezz, 6 avenue Frémiet, 75016 Paris
tel (33) (0)1 56 75 26 26   **fax** (33) (0)1 56 75 26 16
e-mail mail@hotelsezz.com
room rates from €250

absolutely have to see
Bir-Hakeim Bridge: an Art Nouveau riveted-iron masterpiece of engineering in the 16th, and a less heralded combination of sculpture and innovation

must have lunch
Crystal Room, Baccarat, 11 Place des Etats-Unis, 75016 Paris (tel 01 40 22 11 22): dazzling restaurant in a mansion recently refurbished by Philippe Starck for Baccarat, including a museum of their finest historic crystal; a real jewel

First published in 2006 in paperback in the United States of America by
Thames & Hudson Inc., 500 Fifth Avenue, New York, New York 10110

thamesandhudsonusa.com

Library of Congress Catalog Card Number 2005910415

ISBN-13: 978-0-500-28617-3
ISBN-10: 0-500-28617-5

Printed and bound in Singapore by CS Graphics

Designed by Maggi Smith